NASA
and the
Space Race

Keith Gaines

Notes

★ This book uses the American spelling of "center".
The English spelling is "centre".
★ NASA's web sites are frequently updated, so some of the
web pages and addresses in this book may change slightly.

OXFORD
UNIVERSITY PRESS

Great Clarendon Street, Oxford OX2 6DP

Oxford University Press is a department of the University of Oxford.
It furthers the University's objective of excellence in research, scholarship,
and education by publishing worldwide in

Oxford New York

Auckland Bangkok Buenos Aires Cape Town Chennai
Dar es Salaam Delhi Hong Kong Istanbul Karachi Kolkata
Kuala Lumpur Madrid Melbourne Mexico City Mumbai Nairobi
São Paulo Shanghai Singapore Taipei Tokyo Toronto

with an associated company in Berlin

Oxford is a registered trade mark of Oxford University Press
in the UK and in certain other countries

British Library Cataloguing in Publication Data

Data available

ISBN 0 19 917532 2

10 9 8 7 6 5 4 3 2 1

Inspection Pack (nine different titles)   ISBN 0 19 917535 7
Guided Reading Pack (six of the same title)   ISBN 0 19 917855 0
Class Pack ISBN 0 19 917536 5

Acknowledgements

The publisher would like to thank the following for permission to reproduce
photographs:

Corbis UK Ltd: pp 10, 21 (*bottom*), 22; Corbis UK Ltd/Bettmann Archive: pp 14
(*top*), 18 (*top*); Corbis UK Ltd/Franz-Marc Frei: pp 13 (*top*), 23, 24 (*both*); Corbis UK
Ltd/Hulton Deutsch: p 5 (*top right*); Corbis UK Ltd/Richard T Nowitz: p 15 (*top*);
Corbis UK Ltd/Roger Ressmeyer: pp 11 (*bottom*), 21 (*top*); Eumensat: p 26 (*top*);
Keith Gaines: p 4 (*top right, bottom right*); Hulton Getty: pp 4 (*bottom left*), 6 (*top*);
The Moviestore Collection: 12 (*top*); NASA: pp 1, 6 (*bottom*), 7 (*both*), 11 (*top*), 12
(*bottom left and right*), 14 (*bottom*), 18 (*bottom left and right*), 20 (*both*), 25 (*top*), 26
(*bottom*), 27, 32 and back cover; Novosti Photo Library: p 15 (*bottom*); Photodisc:
p 3, 29 (*all*), 30, 31; Science Photo Library: p 5 (*bottom right*).

Artwork is by David Russell. Screen grabs are by Matt Buckley.

Front Cover: NASA

Printed in Hong Kong

Contents

The space race

On 3 October 1942, at a secret base in Germany, SS Major Werner von Braun watched his new A4 **rocket** take off. Germany had been at war for three years. The A4 rocket was made to drop huge bombs on enemy cities.

The Americans, the British and the Russians, who were at war with Germany, were all working on rockets. They were racing against Germany to build powerful rockets that could be guided.

All these rockets were built for war, but when the first A4 was launched, von Braun said to his team, "Do you realize that today the spaceship was born?"

*The first A4 **launch** was a success. This picture is from a film taken in 1942.*

Some A4 launches failed. This old film shows an A4 rocket exploding on take-off.

Von Braun and his team went on to build the V2 rocket. It was the most powerful rocket of its time.

In 1945, at the end of World War II, American soldiers captured the powerful German V2 rockets. They also captured von Braun and his team. The German scientists were taken to the USA.

For the next 12 years, the American army, navy and air force all worked to make a rocket that could go into space. The American rockets became bigger and faster. But on 4 October 1957, the American people were amazed and shocked when a rocket shot into space for the first time. The rocket was Russian!

Von Braun became the chief rocket engineer for the American army.

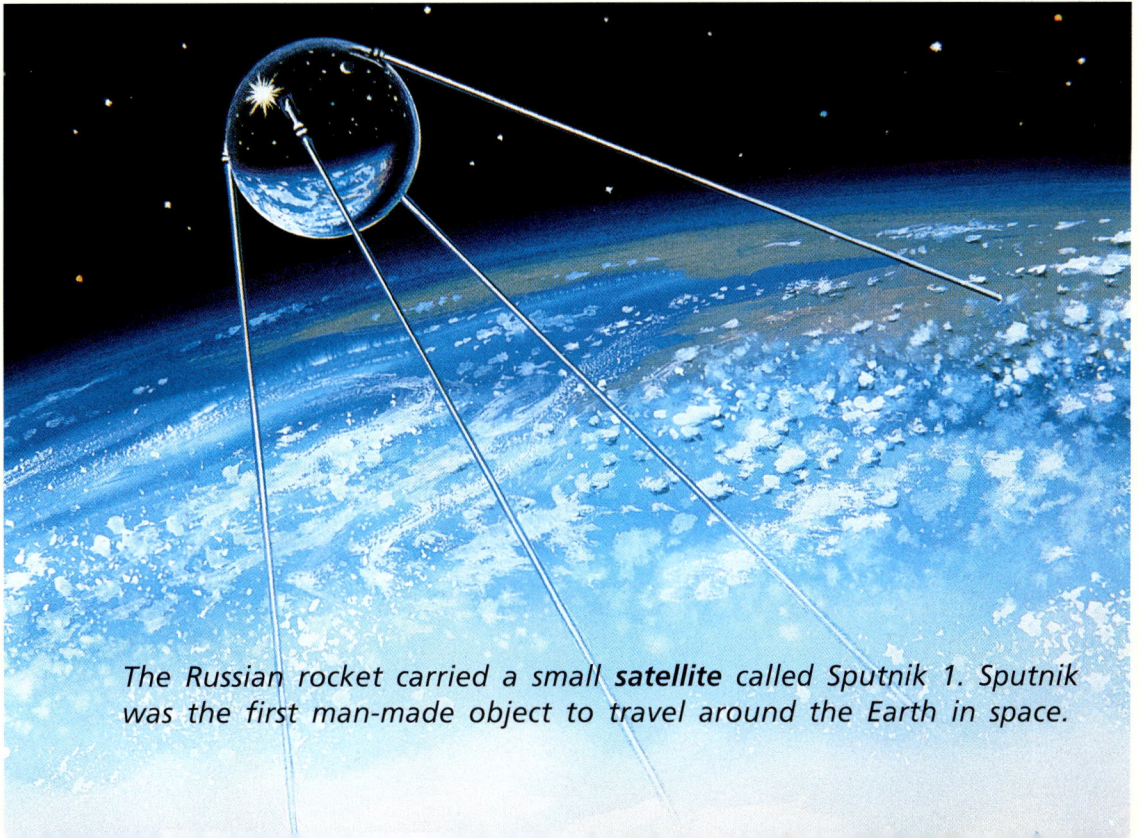

*The Russian rocket carried a small **satellite** called Sputnik 1. Sputnik was the first man-made object to travel around the Earth in space.*

5

The Russians had been working on **rockets** in secret. The Americans were determined to get ahead. In 1958, the American government set up an organization called the National Aeronautics and Space Administration, (**NASA**). NASA's job was to work out how to put machines and people into space, and how to beat the Russians in the "space race".

Over the next 12 years, Russia and the USA made great advances in space travel.

Alexei Leonov was the first man to walk in space.

The space race

1958   The first American space rocket, Explorer 1, goes into space.

1961   Russia puts the first man, Yuri Gagarin, in space.

1962   The first American, John Glenn, orbits earth.

1962   The USA puts the first TV **satellite** into space.

1965   Russian **astronaut**, Alexei Leonov, is the first man to go outside a spacecraft wearing a **spacesuit**.

1966   Russian spacecraft, Luna 9, lands on the Moon.

1969   The USA lands the first men on the Moon, Neil Armstrong and Edwin ("Buzz") Aldrin.

Neil Armstrong and Buzz Aldrin put the American flag on the Moon.

With the first men on the Moon, NASA took the lead in the space race. Today, NASA remains the biggest and most successful space agency in the world.

Main NASA projects

1973	Skylab, the first American **space station** goes into orbit round Earth
1975–1997	Viking and Pathfinder, two robot spacecraft sent to Mars
1977–1990	Voyager, robot spacecraft explore the planets
1981–today	**Space shuttle**, a spacecraft that can be re-used
1990–today	Hubble Space Telescope, a telescope in space
1998–today	International Space Station, a permanent base in space

A launch of the Space shuttle in 1996

The Hubble Space Telescope was the first telescope outside Earth's atmosphere. It can send very clear pictures of distant stars to Earth.

7

Visits to NASA

NASA has many sites in the USA. The rest of this book tells you about some of the sites you can travel to and some of the **web sites** you can visit on your computer.

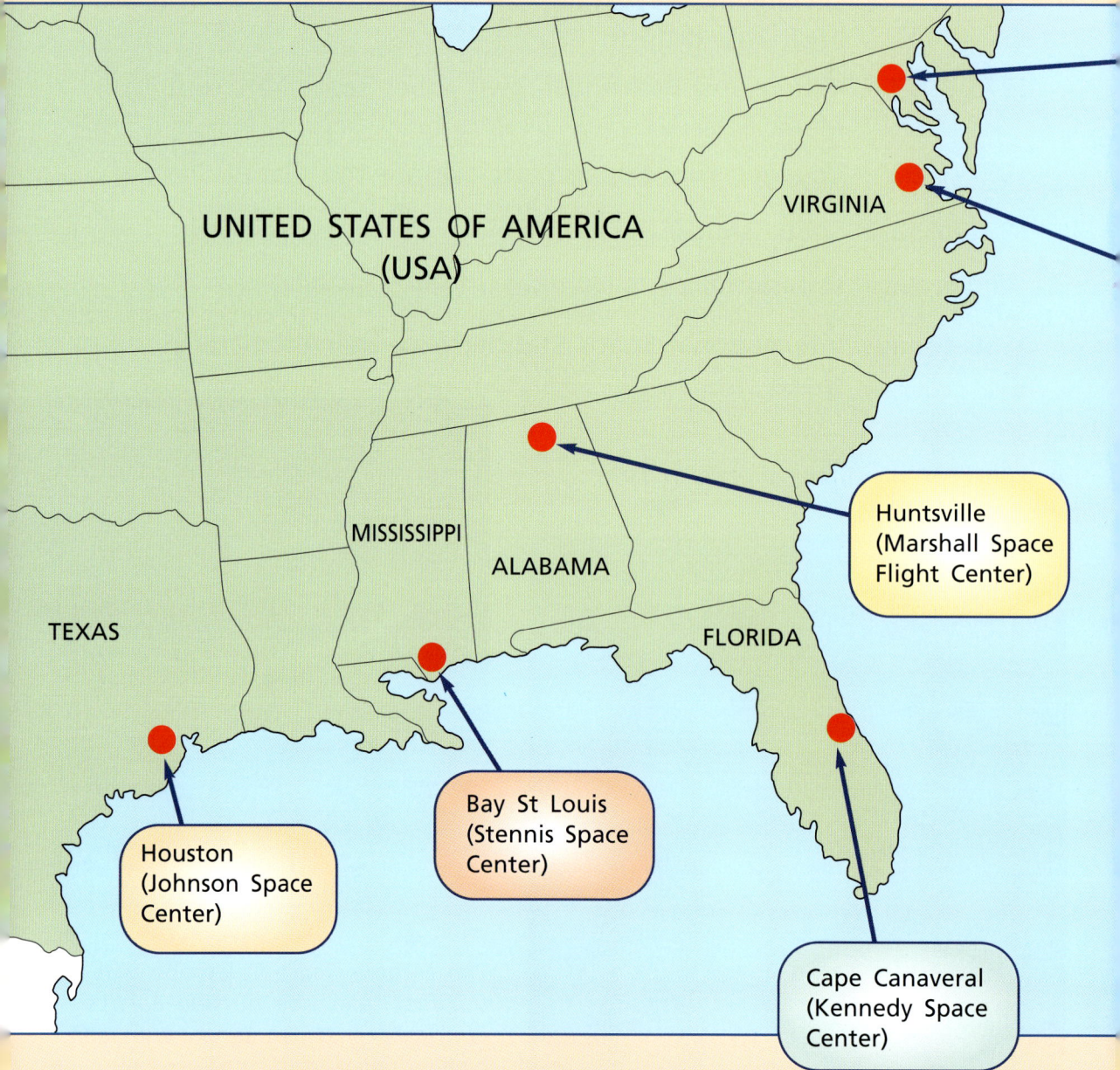

UNITED STATES OF AMERICA
(USA)

VIRGINIA

MISSISSIPPI

ALABAMA

TEXAS

FLORIDA

Huntsville
(Marshall Space
Flight Center)

Bay St Louis
(Stennis Space
Center)

Houston
(Johnson Space
Center)

Cape Canaveral
(Kennedy Space
Center)

CANADA

UNITED STATES OF AMERICA
(USA)

MEXICO

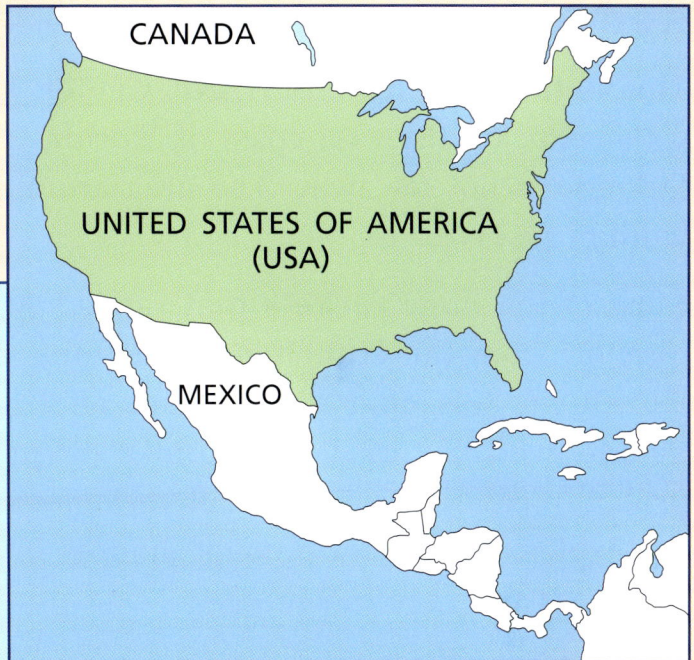

Washington
(National Air and Space
Museum and Goddard
Space Flight Center)

Hampton
(Langley Research Center)

NASA web sites

The main sites are:

Kennedy Space Center: www.kennedyspacecenter.com
Smithsonian / National Air and Space Museum: www.nasm.edu
Johnson Space Center: www.jsc.nasa.gov
Stennis Space Center: www.ssc.nasa.gov
Marshall Space Flight Center: www.msfc.nasa.gov
Goddard Space Flight Center: www.gsfc.nasa.gov
Langley Research Center: www.larc.nasa.gov

Most of these sites have pages for children. Look on the main menus and click on things that interest you.

Kennedy Space Center

www.kennedyspacecenter.com

This is the most famous **NASA** Center. It is at Cape Canaveral, on the east coast of Florida. The holiday town of Orlando is not far away. The area around the Center is a wildlife reserve.

Most of the huge **rockets** that carried Americans into space took off from the **launch pads** at Cape Canaveral. The launch site was built near the sea and in an area where few people lived. If rockets fail to take off properly, they will probably crash into the sea. If rockets explode on take-off, the explosion will not damage houses or people.

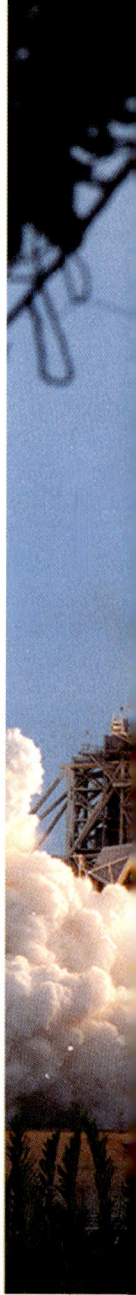

*A **Space shuttle** is taken to the launch pad on a moving platform. The specially-made road is as wide as an eight-lane motorway.*

If you visit the Kennedy Space Center, you can see how a Space shuttle trip is planned. You can walk through a Shuttle orbiter. You can see real Moon rocks and some of the rockets used in the early NASA space flights. Films of past NASA projects are shown on a giant screen.

If you are there at the right time, you can even watch a **launch** from the Kennedy Space Center. The viewing area is about two kilometres away from the shuttle launch pads.

*This rock was picked up on the Moon by **astronauts** on the **Apollo** 15 mission, 1971.*

The Space shuttle Atlantis blasts away from the fixed service structure (on the left), 1992.

Apollo missions

Apollo rockets were used from 1968 to 1972 to explore the Moon. Altogether, there were 17 Apollo missions, but not all were successful.

In 1967, an Apollo **capsule** was being tested on the ground when it caught fire. The three **astronauts** in it were killed.

The film Apollo 13 *tells the story of how the three astronauts survived in the damaged spacecraft.*

The Apollo 13 mission, on its way to the Moon in 1970, almost ended in disaster. An oxygen tank blew up and damaged many of the controls and the **batteries** that powered the instruments and computers. The three astronauts on board used parts of the lunar **module** to build new equipment to keep them alive. In darkness and freezing cold, the astronauts just made it back to Earth.

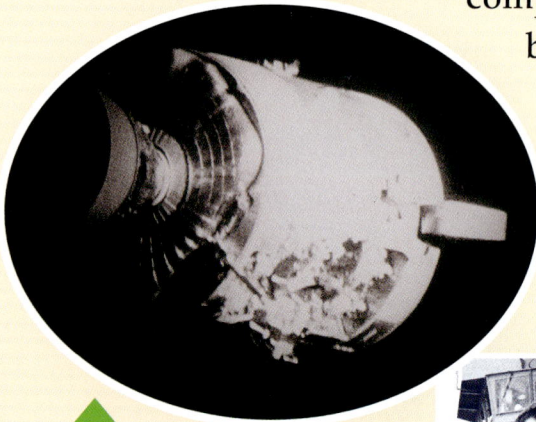

The damaged module on Apollo 13

The Apollo 13 astronauts on board an American ship, which picked them out of the Pacific Ocean at the end of their mission.

Space camps

Every summer, there are week-long camps for children at the Kennedy Space Center. Campers, aged eight to twelve, can take part in experiments that look at the science of space flight.

The children meet engineers and scientists working on current missions. They also build spacecraft models and play games under the giant **Saturn V** rocket.

*Some children try on **spacesuits** during their stay at space camp.*

If you cannot fly to the Kennedy Space Center, you can visit their web site. The full address is www.kennedyspacecenter.com.

National Air and Space Museum

www.nasm.edu

The biggest collection of aircraft and spacecraft in the world is in Washington, the capital city of the USA. It is called the National Air and Space Museum.

The history of flight

If you visit the National Air and Space Museum, you can see the first plane that flew powered by an engine. It was made by two brothers, Orville and Wilbur Wright.

The **exhibits** in this museum show how we have gone from the first plane, flying just a few metres above the ground, to space flights and **space stations**. It has happened in less than 100 years!

The Wright brothers called their plane the Flyer. It made its first flight in 1903.

The Bell X1 was the first aeroplane to travel faster than the speed of sound. (We call this "supersonic".)

14

In the National Air and Space Museum, you can see the original **Apollo** 11 command **module**, which flew to the Moon and back. You can also see aircraft and rockets from other countries, including a Russian SS20 rocket. In 1987, the USA and Russia agreed to ban the use of some nuclear weapons, including the SS20.

The Apollo 11 command module and the Flyer are displayed in the same room.

A Russian SS20 rocket. It could travel halfway round the world, carrying a nuclear bomb.

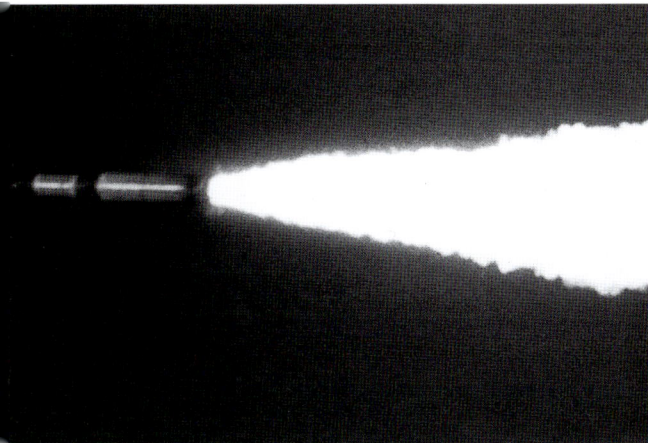

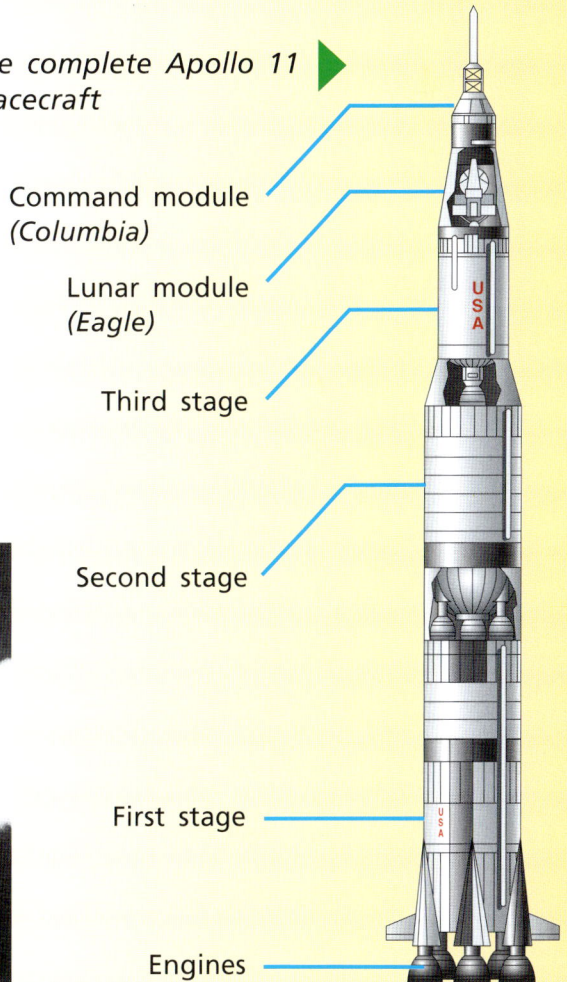

The complete Apollo 11 spacecraft

Command module (Columbia)

Lunar module (Eagle)

Third stage

Second stage

First stage

Engines

On the National Air and Space Musem **web site**, there is a section called "**Apollo** to the Moon" (www.nasm.si.edu/galleries/attm/enter.html). In this section, you can read about the space race and all the Apollo missions. You can also see some of the **exhibits** on display at the museum.

section heading

sub-section

main text

exhibit in museum

menu

The Smithsonian

The National Air and Space Museum is just one of the museums which make up the huge Smithsonian Museum.

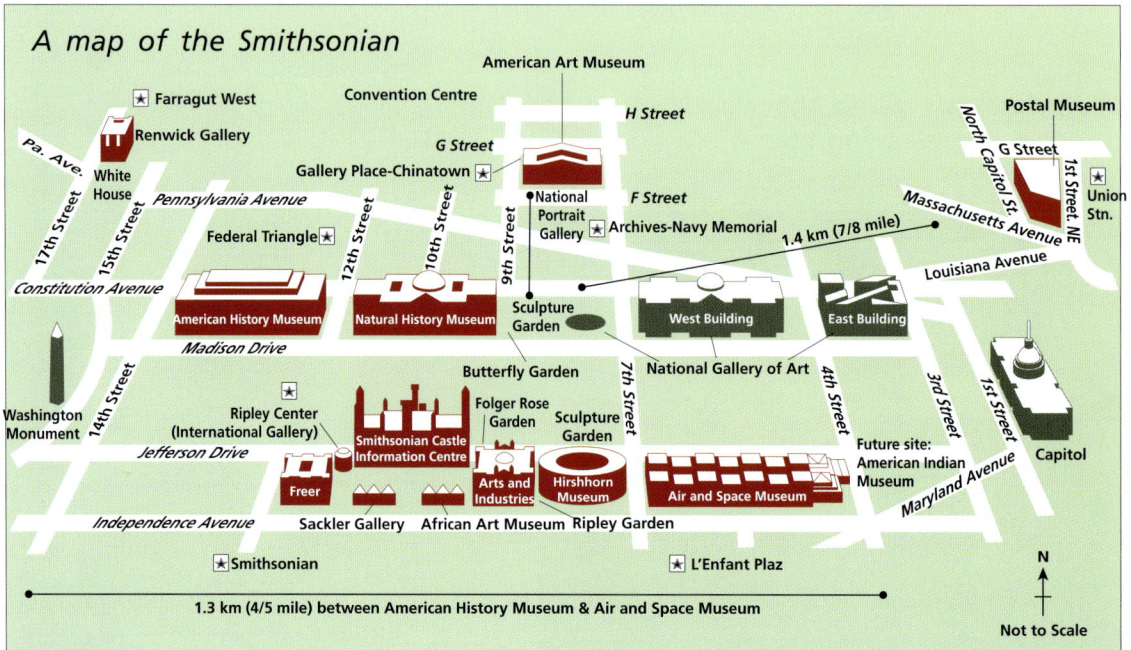

A map of the Smithsonian

Farragut West
Renwick Gallery
Pa. Ave.
White House
Pennsylvania Avenue
Federal Triangle
Constitution Avenue
17th Street
15th Street
American History Museum
Madison Drive
Washington Monument
14th Street
Ripley Center (International Gallery)
Jefferson Drive
Freer
Independence Avenue
Sackler Gallery
Smithsonian

Convention Centre
American Art Museum
H Street
G Street
Gallery Place-Chinatown
12th Street
10th Street
National Portrait Gallery
9th Street
F Street
Archives-Navy Memorial
Natural History Museum
Sculpture Garden
Butterfly Garden
Smithsonian Castle Information Centre
Folger Rose Garden
Arts and Industries
African Art Museum
Hirshhorn Museum
Sculpture Garden
Ripley Garden
7th Street
National Gallery of Art
West Building
Air and Space Museum
L'Enfant Plaz

1.4 km (7/8 mile)
Massachusetts Avenue
Louisiana Avenue
East Building
4th Street
Future site: American Indian Museum
Maryland Avenue
North Capitol St.
G Street
Postal Museum
1st Street, NE
Union Stn.
3rd Street
1st Street
Capitol

N

1.3 km (4/5 mile) between American History Museum & Air and Space Museum

Not to Scale

16

Project Apollo Drawings and Technical Diagrams

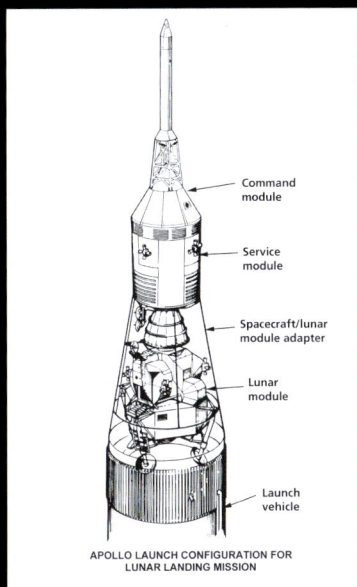

APOLLO LAUNCH CONFIGURATION FOR
LUNAR LANDING MISSION

**Apollo Spacecraft Launch
Configuration**

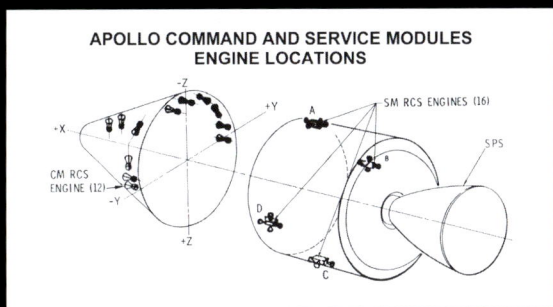

Apollo Command and Service Modules and Launch Escape System

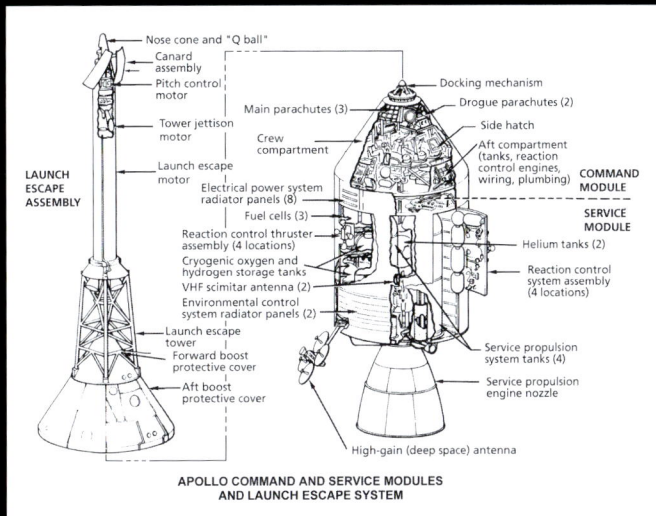

APOLLO COMMAND AND SERVICE MODULES
AND LAUNCH ESCAPE SYSTEM

APOLLO COMMAND AND SERVICE MODULES
ENGINE LOCATIONS

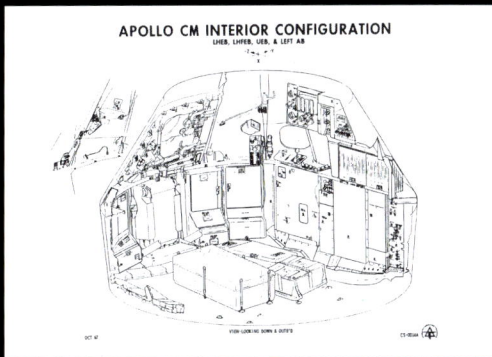

Command and Service Module Engine Locations

APOLLO CM INTERIOR CONFIGURATION

Apollo Spacecraft/LM Adapter

Building a space rocket

Have you ever wanted to build your own space rocket?
You can look up plans for the Apollo project at
www.hq.nasa.gov/office/pao/History/diagrams/apollo.

Johnson Space Center

www.jsc.nasa.gov

The Johnson Space Center is in the city of Houston, in Texas. It is the control center for many space flights.

Ground control

Each space mission has a **flight controller** in charge, who talks to the **astronauts**. Teams of people support each mission, checking the condition of the spacecraft and the astronauts.

In the mission control room at Houston, a big screen shows live pictures of astronauts on their way to the Moon.

During the **Apollo** missions, the astronauts had instruments taped to their bodies that measured their **temperature**, their **heartbeat** and other signs of how well they were. The measurements were sent to Houston Control by radio and studied by doctors during the flight.

A doctor in Houston studies measurements from an astronaut's body.

An astronaut in space is monitored to check his health.

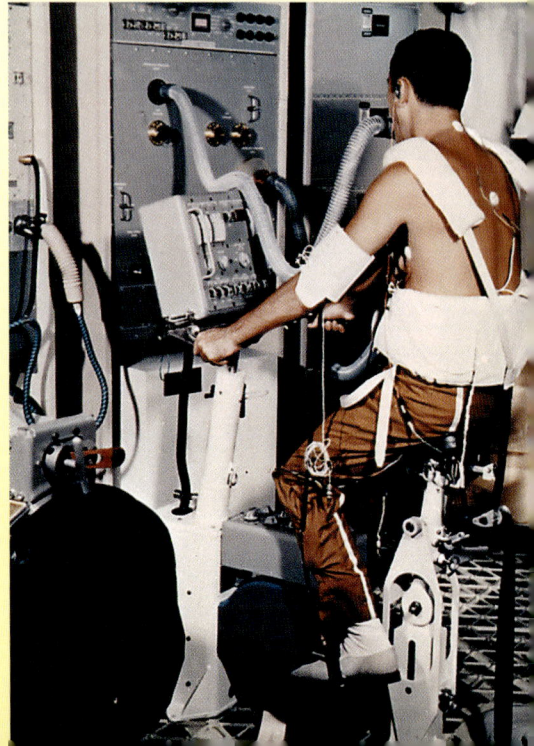

Instruments in the spacecraft also measured the quality and pressure of the air, how much electricity was in the **batteries**, and the position of the spacecraft. All this information was radioed to Houston and studied by the ground crew.

Space news

At the Johnson Space Center **web site**, you can get news of the latest space flights. You can read about the astronauts who are in space now, or who will be on the next mission. You can also learn about how the new International **Space Station** is being built.

News of the latest events in space can be found on www.jsc.nasa.gov. *Click on Hot Topics and then on Human Space Flight.*

There is even a space toy shop and an astronaut ice cream shop on this web site!

Astronaut ice-cream for sale on www.nasastore.jsc.nasa.gov/bigpicts/icecream.

Stennis Space Center

www.ssc.nasa.gov

The Stennis Space Center is in Mississippi. It is where **NASA**'s rocket **engines** are tested.

All the engines for the **Space shuttle** have to pass a series of tests at the center. These engines have to blast the Space shuttle out of the Earth's atmosphere.

Space stations

Scientists at the Stennis Space Center are developing powerful engines that can carry heavy materials into space to build the new International **Space Station**. Sixteen countries are working together to build this space station, which will circle the Earth.

This is what the International Space Station will look like when it is finished.

Over 40 **launches** will be made over five years, taking hundreds of pieces into space. The pieces will be put together to make a **laboratory** in space, where people can work on scientific and medical experiments.

A Space shuttle engine is held in a frame and fired to test for any problems.

Three space stations have orbited Earth. The first was Salyut 1, launched by Russia in 1971. The second was Skylab, the American space station. It was launched in 1973. These space stations were small so there was little room on board to carry out experiments. Neither of them are still in space.

The third, and biggest, space station was launched by Russia. It was called Mir, which is the Russian word for "peace". The first part of Mir was launched in 1986.

Skylab *space station. It was in Earth's orbit from 1973 to 1979.*

The Russian space station, Mir, *in orbit above Earth.*

When the space stations wore out, rockets were fired to send them back to Earth. Mir finally crashed to Earth in 2001, after 15 years in space.

Marshall Space Flight Center

www.msfc.nasa.gov

At this site in Huntsville, Alabama, scientists worked on early American **rockets**. These rockets were made as weapons, like the V2 rocket (pages 4 and 5) and not as spacecraft. After World War II, the Americans and Russians feared that their countries would be at war with each other, so they made bigger and faster rockets to carry bombs.

Werner von Braun (see pages 4 and 5) and his team worked at the Huntsville site. They developed **missiles**, such as the Redstone surface-to-surface missile, which was first launched in 1953. The rocket for this missile was later used to take an American **astronaut**, Alan Shepherd, on a short trip to the outer edge of the Earth's atmosphere.

A Trident missile is fired from an American submarine in 1982, during a test.

As well as working on missiles, the team at the Marshall Space Flight Center worked on spacecraft. They tested the **Saturn V** rockets which took the American astronauts to the Moon. One reporter watched a test. He said, "It was total flame, total sound, total power." The noise of the blast could be heard over 80 kilometres away.

Today, the Marshall Space Flight Center still works on space projects, such as the International **Space Station** and the development of future space vehicles. It also has a large museum and park for visitors.

Museum and park

In the park you can see many old missiles and rockets. You can even walk beside a full stack shuttle. This is a **Space shuttle** complete with the fuel tank and booster rocket.

A full stack shuttle

There are many amazing rides at the Marshall Space Flight Center. On the Space Shot ride, you go over 40 metres up into the air – but you do it in two and a half seconds! You are pressed back into your seat, just like an **astronaut** on take-off. Then you come down so quickly that you float freely for two seconds, like an astronaut in space.

▲ A ride in the Multi-Axis gyro whirls you round so fast that your body is three times its normal weight.

You can also sit inside an **Apollo** cockpit trainer, which was used to train astronauts to fly the Apollo spacecraft. You can make a virtual landing on the Moon and you can even take a virtual ride across the surface of Mars!

◀ At the Marshall Space Flight Center you can see just how big an Apollo **rocket** really is.

Liftoff to Learning

On the **web site** for the Marshall Space Flight Center, there is a section called Liftoff to Learning. Click on this to find out more about rockets, **satellites**, research in space, and life on a **space station**.

Today, astronauts can spend weeks or even months in space, so the space station is their home. The station gets electricity from solar panels and all water has to be recycled. Look on the web site to find out about sleeping in space, eating in space and even how you use a toilet in space!

Astronaut, Jack Lousma, takes a bath on Skylab. The shower curtain is pulled up from the floor and fixed to the ceiling. Water is drawn through the showerhead by a vacuum system.

There are many on-line space games on the web site.

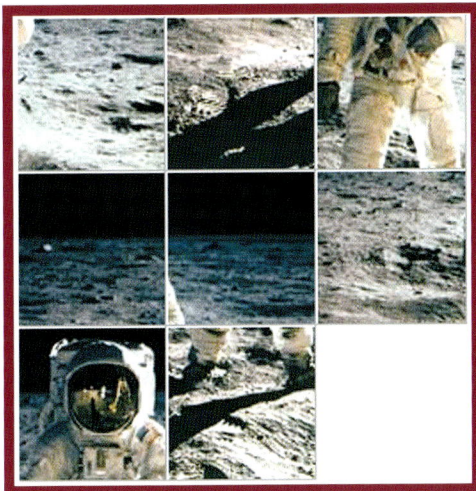

Could you slide these tiles around, one at a time, to make the full picture?

Goddard Space Flight Center

A short drive out of Washington will bring you to the Goddard Space Flight Center. At this Center, scientists use information from spacecraft and **satellites** in space to find out about the Earth.

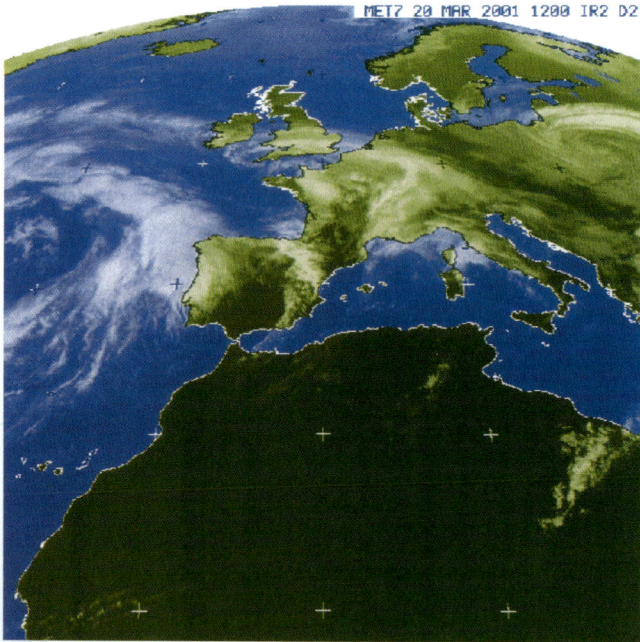

MET7 20 MAR 2001 1200 IR2 D2

Today, there are many satellites orbiting the Earth. They send down information and photos 24 hours a day. Satellite photos are often used on TV weather forecasts.

This picture of Europe and north Africa was taken by satellite. The thick white clouds bring rain and strong winds.

Doctor Robert H. Goddard was one of the first Americans to make **rockets**. The Goddard Space Flight Center is named after him.

Dr Goddard about to launch the first liquid-fuelled rocket, in 1926.

Langley Research Center

www.larc.nasa.gov

Langley Research Center opened in 1917, just 14 years after the first aeroplane flight (see page 14). It was the USA's first aeroplane **laboratory**.

To find out more about how aeroplanes worked, the Langley Center built **wind tunnels**. Aircraft are still tested in wind tunnels today. Parts or models of aircraft are hung inside the wind tunnels and air is blown over them (as if they are in flight). Scientists can study the effect it has on them.

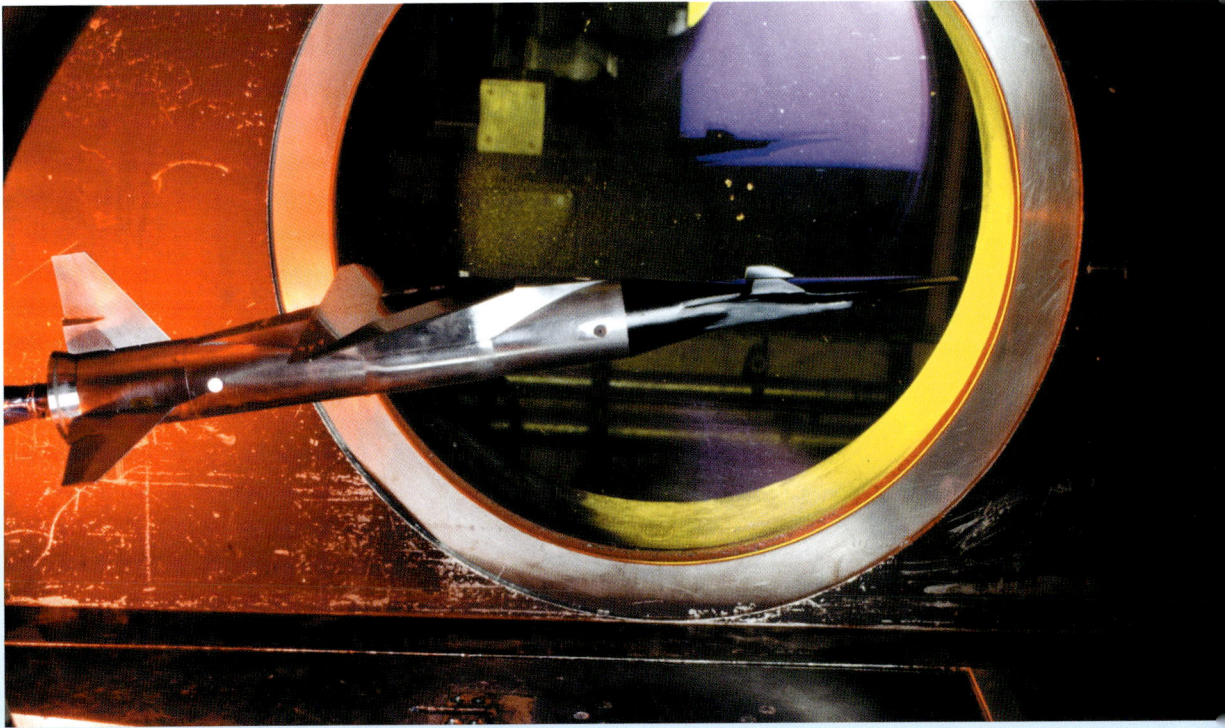

In 1958, Langley was used as the training centre for America's first **astronauts**. Langley still works mainly on testing aeroplanes, but it is also working on the design of future spacecraft that will replace the shuttle.

Aircraft are still tested in wind tunnels today.

NASA for kids

NASA has thousands of web pages, but look out for the web pages that are for children. "NASA for Kids" is one of the best **web sites**. You can download and watch films of **rocket launches**. You can use their suggestions for your own flight experiments! Search for "NASA for Kids", or type in www.nasa.gov/kids.

To find out about some of the planets in the **solar system**, click on the green planet, then click "solar system", then "planets".

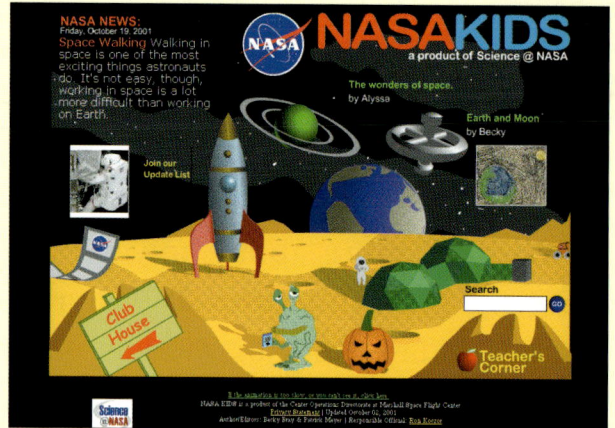

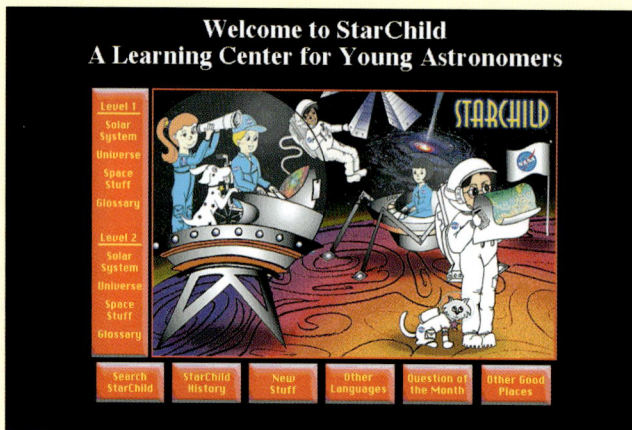

"Starchild" is another good NASA web site for children. You can find it at www.starchild.gsfc.nasa.gov. This web site tells you all about stars, comets, black holes, and much more. It even tells you how you can become an **astronaut**.

▲

Jupiter is a stormy planet. It has 27 moons. Some of these moons are covered in ice. Others are covered in hot lava.

▲

Saturn has bright rings around its middle. These rings are made up of small bits of rock and ice.

▲

Neptune, the blue planet, is named after the Roman god of the sea. It travels round the Sun once every 165 years.

▲

Mars is the planet most like Earth. It has polar ice caps, volcanoes, mountains and valleys.

Glossary

Apollo American project to put men on the moon

astronauts people who go into space

batteries units for storing electricity for instruments, computers, lights, etc.

booster rockets rockets fixed beside a main rocket, which fall off when all the fuel is burned

capsule small spacecraft sent out from a bigger spacecraft

exhibit something shown in public

flight controller person in overall charge of a space flight

heartbeat the rate or speed at which the heart beats

laboratory place where people carry out experiments and research

launch when a rocket takes off

launch pad place from which a rocket takes off, e.g. at Cape Canaveral

missile rocket-powered bomb which travels high in the air

module small part of a spacecraft made to detach from bigger part, e.g. "lunar module", made to land on Moon then return to spacecraft; "command module", small top part of spacecraft which returns astronauts to Earth

NASA the National Aeronautics and Space Administration of the USA

rocket tube filled with explosive material which burns to make gas which pushes the tube forwards

satellite any object that goes around another object, e.g. the Moon is a satellite of the Earth

Saturn V huge rocket used for all the American Moon missions

Skylab the first American space station to orbit round Earth

solar system the planets and other objects that are satellites of our Sun

Space shuttle spacecraft that is carried into space by rocket, but which lands like an aeroplane and can be re-used

space station man-made building in space, e.g. Skylab, Salyut and Mir

spacesuit suit which an astronaut wears in space or on the Moon. Spacesuits have their own air supply and heating

temperature how hot or cold something is

web site pages of text, pictures and sometimes sound and moving pictures which can be seen on the internet through a computer

wind tunnel tunnel made with giant fans at one end which blow air through the tunnel, usually to test aircraft

Index